Come All Ye Faithful

Three Christmas Plays

Frank Ramirez

CSS Publishing Company, Inc., Lima, Ohio

COME ALL YE FAITHFUL

For more information about CSS Publishing Company resources, visit our website at www.csspub.com or email us at csr@csspub.com or call (800) 241-4056.

Cover design by Barbara Spencer
ISBN-13: 978-0-7880-2485-6
ISBN-10: 0-7880-2485-X

PRINTED IN USA

To my brother
Timothy John Ramirez
artist and musician
who is pretty dramatic himself

Table Of Contents

Introduction

Part of the central core of the Christian confession is the proclamation in John 1:14: "The Word was made flesh and dwelt among us."

In the theater, words are made flesh, and come alive in our midst. In some ways, theater provides an extraordinary paradigm for the business of church and God's people. Yet, historically the church, at least the established church, has been at the least uncomfortable and often out and out antagonistic toward the theater.

I wonder if that has always been the case? When the apostle Paul tells us "Do not be deceived: 'Bad company ruins good morals' " (1 Corinthians 15:33), he is not quoting from Old Testament scripture. He is quoting from the comic playwright, Menander, the founder of the modern situation comedy, and a writer so popular that phrases from his comedies were part of ordinary speech.

Paul also uses images from the theater. Although the acoustics in ancient Greek theaters were nothing short of extraordinary, crowds numbering in the tens of thousands meant that many people sat too far away to read facial expressions. Actors wore oversized masks to portray complex emotions. Paul used the word for these masks, known as *hupocritese*, as an image for those he called "hypocrites," people wearing emotions on their face for show.

A document attributed to the second-century Christian writer, Justin Martyr, consists of little more than quotations from Greek comedy and tragedy, using well-known lines to demonstrate that throughout time, even pagan literature has been pointing to Jesus! Certainly, Paul and the other early Christians knew their theater well enough to quote.

I mentioned earlier the verse, John 1:14: "The Word was made flesh and dwelt among us." The Greek word for "dwelt," *skene*, is the word for "tent," and alludes at the least to the tabernacle in the desert, which was not a permanent structure, but could be moved around as needed.

This is crucial. You can't pin the Word down. It's moving. Moreover, the Word is tenting among us, roughing it among us. That is intended as a model for the life of the Christian as well.

Just as the Word is made flesh, so words are made flesh in our lives together as believers. In the sermon, words put flesh on biblical concepts to make them come alive. The Word of God is made flesh when the holy command for justice and righteousness come alive in our lives. Certainly the Living Word lives in our midst when we kneel and wash each other's feet as brethren.

That word, *skene*, is not only crucial theologically, but theatrically as well. The English word, "scene," comes from *skene*, and thus the latter is the root for the theatrical backdrops that were tentlike structures used for the medieval mystery plays that told the biblical story from Genesis to Revelation, and which today might be flats, curtains, or other scenery.

The theater is the most incarnational of arts, and yet is one of the most mistrusted by the church. Preachers in many ages have railed against the stage as the corrupter of youth, and the despoiler of women's virtues.

The theater is certainly a dangerous art, especially if you are one who treasures the status quo. In most ages, clothes defined the person. Eras that believed there was something qualitatively different about noble and commoner insisted that you only wear the clothes of your station. Yet, actors wore the clothing of all stations. The same actor (usually male) might be a man or a woman, an elder or a youth, a nobleman or a pauper, and pull the part of well enough to fool everyone. This is frightening to those at the upper reaches of society, whose welfare depends on the poor accepting their lot.

Christians gathered, slave and free, male and female, rich and poor, Jew and Gentile, at the same table in a way that scandalized the Roman Empire. Certainly, we who don robes to descend into the river to be made a new creation will gladly accept the transformation that comes as actors don costumes and turn our world upside down.

But we don't. Christians have often wanted a tightly controlled, safe, didactic, and pious theater. The church distrusts the theater.

I have noticed in recent years some thawing of the relationship. Though I was a theater arts major in college and have been active in community theater since graduation, I have not often been involved with church drama until recently.

That's in part because some church dramas tend to be stiff, wooden, and so concerned with preserving a false and unbiblical propriety that the urgent reality of scripture, or the lessons to be learned from it, are lost.

The past eight years or so I've begun to write dramas for the church. The pieces I write are largely light (with a few exceptions), but they are written with the intent of presenting the truth of God's word with little words. Some of these dramas may be found in the collections *The Christmas Star*, *Gabriel's Horn*, *The Bee Attitudes*, and the play "M.I.H. Missing In Heaven," from the Easter anthology, *Roll Back The Stone*. All of these titles are available from CSS Publishing Company.

These particular plays came about through requests. Our children's choir wanted dramas for the Christmas season, and there came a request from one of our musicians for something a little more dramatic to go with "The Living Advent Wreath." I try to make plays to be presented in worship as simple as possible, and encourage the use of script in hand, because so much energy can be spent in memorization that the intent of the play can be lost.

I thank everyone who originally took part in these little plays. For "The Living Advent Wreath," that would be Mari Hawbaker (Pilgrim), Jessica Hann (Faith), Kasey Leidy (Hope), David Wilt (Love), Wilma Morse (Magi), Carol Cooper (Magi), Leah Pepple (Magi), and as accompanist, Alyssa Harclerode. I directed and played the Guide. Janelle Cogan created the original artistic design. In "The Mouse Christmas," Garrison Leonard, Vanessa Leonard, Olivia Hillenbrand, Taylor Hillenbrand, Alexis Calhoun, Krystal Morse, and Morgan Knepp as the mice were joined by Alyssa Harclerode as the grandmother. Allegra Morral and Prudy Wilt directed and provided the accompaniment. "The Ad Vent Wheat" included Alex Calhoun, Alexis Calhoun, Bradley Knepp, Olivia Hillenbrand, Krystal Morse, Kristin Caro, Courtney Caro, and Garrison Leonard, who were joined by their directors, Allegra Morral and Prudy Wilt, who played the two teachers.

Living Advent Wreath

A♭ Gm Fm7 E♭
Sweet - ly for spring and her nur - tur - ing show - er.
Not while the Moon shines to call the for - lorn. Sing!
Love sees a pat - tern, and so like the weav - er,
Still we must seize what our his - to - ry of - fers.
E♭ Cm7 Fm7 B♭
Faith I am. Snow a - bounds. Burn.
Shine in the dark - ness, till hark,
Col - ors bright bind us in plaits.
Star in the East lights the way.
E♭ Cm B♭7 E♭ E♭sus4 E♭
Sun - shine will al - ways re - turn.
Day has re - turned. hear the lark.
Pa - tient - ly bid - ing, Love waits.
Moon and Sun too have their say.

MAGI

Living Advent Wreath

Text: Frank Ramirez

Music: Steve Engle

A♭ Gm Fm7 E♭
Still we must seize what our his - to - ry of - fers.
unis. E♭ Cm7 Fm7 B♭
Star in the East lights the way.
(Star lights the way.)
E♭ Cm B♭7 E♭ E♭sus4 E♭
(melody)
Moon and Sun too have their say.
(Too have their say.)

Living Advent Wreath-5.

A♭ Gm Fm7 E♭ G7 Cm9 Cm
Peace can be found with the babe in the man - ger.
E♭ Cm7 Fm7 B♭
Fath, Hope, and Love all a - gree.
E♭ Cm B♭7 E♭ E♭sus4 E♭
Come to the man - ger and see.

Material Used Through Five Weeks

The Living Advent Wreath

Note

Pilgrim and Guide have minimal singing parts. Attendant carries the candlelighter and lights the candles in the Advent wreath each week. Faith, Hope, Love, and Trust, representing the four candles of the Advent wreath, enter one per week, then remain through the final weeks. They have mostly singing parts. Mary, Joseph, and Infant have nonspeaking parts and are seated behind a curtain in the final week of presentation.

Cast

Pilgrim
Guide
Attendant
Faith
Hope
Love
Trust (three people)
Mary
Joseph
Infant

Props

Brown "leaves"
Bare tree
Empty sack
Candlelighter
Advent wreath with candles
Scrolls
Model of the nativity
Star
Flower
Heart

Costumes

Faith wears a purple robe or shirt with the sun on it
Hope wears a purple robe or shirt with the moon on it
Love wears a pink robe or shirt with stars on it
Trust (three people) wears purple robes or shirts with the magi symbols on them
Pilgrim, Guide, and Attendant wear appropriate clothing
Mary, Joseph, and Infant should be as characters in the nativity

Music

The music is provided in this book and will be used throughout this play.

Week 1
First Week of Advent
Faith: Purple Candle of the Sun

The Living Advent Wreath

(Brown leaves are strewn over the floor. There is a bare tree. Pilgrim enters carrying an empty sack.)

Pilgrim: *(picks up leaf and allows it to fall)* There is nothing here. I have traveled many miles on an errand of the king, and so far I have found nothing to take back to him. There is nothing in this bag. There is nothing in my heart.

(Guide, Attendant, and Faith enter. Faith, the first candle of the living Advent wreath, bears a mark of the sun. Attendant, who will light the Advent candles, carries the candlelighter.)

Guide: You look a sight! Greetings, Pilgrim!

Pilgrim: *(startled)* Who are you?

Guide: I am a citizen of this far country, where you seem to find yourself a stranger. And I am a guide to all strangers who find their way here. Are you in need of a guide?

Pilgrim: I'm in need of something. My bag is empty.

Guide: And so is your heart. *(reassures Pilgrim)* No, I can't read minds. I heard you speaking aloud. That is why I came forward.

Pilgrim: Perhaps you can help me.

Guide: Tell me how.

Pilgrim: I have come from a far country. I have come from the king.

Guide: I know.

Pilgrim: How could you know?

Guide: *(smiles)* Every country is far from here. That is why we call this place the Far Country. And every country far from here has a king. What does your king desire? Why are you sent?

Pilgrim: Not long ago, but long ago because of my travels, I was standing in the court of our king when he complained.

Guide: What is his complaint?

Pilgrim: Actually, he has five complaints. We were all standing in the court one day when he did not show up. Normally he arrives with his great retinue. There is a great deal of pageantry when he arrives on the scene.

Guide: *(softly)* Isn't there always?

Pilgrim: Pardon me?

Guide: For what?

Pilgrim: I meant, what did you say? I couldn't hear you.

Guide: Then you must say what you mean. I am not surprised that your king likes pageantry. It is the way this world's kings inflate their self-importance.

Pilgrim: Our king is very important!

Guide: Of course he is. They all are.

Pilgrim: Don't you people have a king?

Guide: Most certainly! He is a powerful king.

Pilgrim: Where is he?

Guide: He is not here yet. He is coming. We are waiting!

Pilgrim: I don't understand.

Guide: Yet, you will. But you were telling me your king arrives with pageantry.

Pilgrim: Yes. He is preceded by fifteen wise men. How many precede your king?

Guide: Three. But they haven't arrived yet.

Pilgrim: Then how can they serve your king?

Guide: He hasn't arrived yet. But he will. Now, please, please, tell me more.

Pilgrim: Yes. The fifteen wise men. Then ladies of the court. Twenty of them. Sometimes thirty. And minstrels, playing lute and lyre, harp and viol, and singing his praises. Finally, the children of the kingdom, ten of them selected from among the best behaved, come before him dropping flower petals. And then the king himself arrives to take his throne to a great fanfare of trumpets. And so it goes all the day long. Every action, every word, is preceded by a great pageant as people of great significance and magnificence perform exact and exacting ceremonies all around him. It is a great and glorious sight!

Guide: It sounds impressive — after a fashion. But something must be wrong. Something must have happened.

Pilgrim: Yes, yes. That is why I am here. On a day not long ago, the wise men arrived, and the ladies of the court, and the minstrels singing his praises, and the children tossing their flower petals. Musicians blew the trumpets. But nothing happened. There was no king. He did not arrive.

Guide: What did you do?

Pilgrim: Nothing at first. We stood there, silent, afraid to move. But, at last, one of the children spoke. The child said ...

Attendant: The king is ill. Come to the king's bed.

Pilgrim: *(amazed)* How did you know that?

Attendant: *(shrugs)* That's the way kings talk.

Guide: So what did you do then?

Pilgrim: We ran to the king, all of us — wise men, ladies, minstrels, children, and all the people of the court, all the courtiers. The grand ones and the bland ones. The tall ones and the small ones. The great ones and the late ones. We burst into the king's chambers and found him lying in bed, barely able to move. We asked him to rise. We begged him to rise. We pled with him. But, he was unable to rise. So we asked him what was wrong. He said, "I have five complaints, five woes that have laid me low. The world is dying. The world is dark. The world is lost. The world is skeptical. The world is war. It seems to me that there is no hope. And this thought lays me low. Is there anyone who will contradict me? Is there anyone who will cheer me?"

Guide: And what did people say?

Pilgrim: What could they say? We are so used to agreeing with the king that, at first, no one said anything. And as he spoke, we all felt the darkness. Then the king pointed to me. He told me to take a bag and travel to a far country and find five things to answer his five complaints. His five woes. The world is dying. The world is dark. The world ...

Guide: Yes, the world is lost. The world is skeptical. The world is war. *(pauses, as if thinking)* Perhaps we can help you. Look all around you. What do you see that is living?

Pilgrim: *(picks up a brown leaf)* What can I see? The leaf is dead. The tree is dead.

Guide: *(laughs)* No, no, no. The leaf is not dead. It is fallen, and it will give life. The tree is not dead. This is autumn and it has begun its long and deep winter's sleep. We are so obsessed with dying that we forget there is a blessing. During autumn and winter, we come to a standstill. The snow covers the earth with a blanket, and nature rests. But never forget that the memory of spring is hidden in the bulbs planted deep beneath the surface of the earth. You can't see the bulbs, but when the spring returns and the hungry sun wakes the ground then the bulbs will send forth the flowers and life returns. We are waiting for a certain future of bounty and love. The world is not dead. The world is alive. Hope is alive.

Pilgrim: How can hope be alive?

Guide: Have faith.

(Faith steps forward to take the place of the first candle in the living Advent wreath as Attendant lights the candle on the altar's Advent wreath.)

Faith: *(sings)*
Faith is the hub at the heart of the flower
While in the autumn she yearns
Sweetly for spring and her nurturing shower.
Faith I am. Snow abounds. Burn.
Sunshine will always return.

Pilgrim: I see! I see! Here is one thing I can bring back to the king. Let me dig up a bulb and take it back to him.

Guide: If you dig up the bulb, it will never flower.

Pilgrim: Then what can I show the king?

Guide: Take the king your faith. Trust the sun. Trust in faith. Your bag must remain empty, but take this wisdom back with you: "... faith is the assurance of things hoped for, the conviction of things not seen" (Hebrews 11:1).

Pilgrim: *(repeats slowly)* "... faith is the assurance of things hoped for, the conviction of things not seen." *(pauses)* So the world is not dying. That answers one of the king's questions. But how about the others? That the world is dark. The world is lost. The world is skeptical. The world is war.

Guide: Please — let faith give you hope. Take rest now. Come to the castle.

Pilgrim: What castle?

Guide: Look with the eyes of faith. It is just beyond that hill. Rest there. And come back. Come back again, and we will see what we can do about your other complaints. For now, think on faith, and have hope.

Faith: *(sings once more)*
Faith is the hub at the heart of the flower
While in the autumn she yearns
Sweetly for spring and her nurturing shower.
Faith I am. Snow abounds. Burn.
Sunshine will always return.

The End

Week 2
Second Week of Advent
Hope: Purple Candle of the Moon

The Living Advent Wreath

(Pilgrim enters to find Faith in the living Advent wreath. Pilgrim still carries the empty bag.)

Pilgrim: Are you still here? Where is the Guide?

(Guide enters with Attendant and Hope. Hope, the second candle of the living Advent wreath, bears the mark of the Moon. Attendant carries the candlelighter.)

Guide: Here I am! Pilgrim, I am glad you have returned.

Pilgrim: I had to. Thanks to you, I have faith. I have faith that even as winter approaches, the sun will return.

Faith: *(sings)*
Faith is the hub at the heart of the flower
While in the autumn she yearns
Sweetly for spring and her nurturing shower.
Faith I am. Snow abounds. Burn.
Sunshine will always return.

Guide: And you remember what I said about faith?

Pilgrim: Faith is the assurance of things hoped for, the conviction of things not seen. Yes, I remember. I have thought on those words. But still, I think of my king, the king in a country far away, who lies dying in his bed because of his fears.

Guide: Do you think he is truly dying?

Pilgrim: He seemed most heart struck to me!

Guide: Then why did he not come himself, do you suppose?

Pilgrim: Kings don't go on their own errands. They send others for them.

Guide: *(laughs)* I am forgetting. We are speaking about the kings of the world again. It is very hard for them to come and to go, to fetch and to carry, and to bear for many ...

Pilgrim: What sort of king comes on his own? What would people think of such a king?

Guide: What would they think, indeed.

Pilgrim: You know, I have looked for *your* king. I have asked after your king. But everyone in the castle seems to know the king, yet has not seen him.

Guide: We have faith. And our king is different than any other. Our king is coming.

Pilgrim: How do you know?

Guide: How can we not know? Look around you.

Pilgrim: I have looked around. And so has our king. That is why he was brought low. He said, "The world is dying. The world is dark. The world is lost. The world is skeptical. The world is war." Now you have taught me the world is not dying. But still, the world is dark. The sun is visible less and less each day. The sun sets earlier and earlier, rises later and later. The world *is* dark. And my bag is still empty.

Guide: Yes, your bag. Your king asked you to bring back five things.

Pilgrim: Five things to answer his complaints. To prove to him the world is not dying, the world is not dark, the world is not lost, the world is not skeptical, and the world is not war. You have taught me that the world is not dying, yet you forbid me from taking a bulb from beneath the earth in order to prove to the king that there is hope. All I have is a song.

Guide: But if you took the bulb you would have neither spring nor hope. Yet, your hope is weak. We must build it up. The sun is setting and the world seems dark. So look to the sky — see the bright moon!

(Hope steps forward to take the place of the second candle in the living Advent wreath as Attendant lights the first and second candles in the altar's Advent wreath.)

Hope: *(sings)*
Dusk is erased with no hint of a morning.
Shall Hope be lost in the dark?
Not while the Moon shines to call the forlorn. Sing!
Shine in the darkness, till hark,
Day has returned, hear the lark.

Guide: Do you hear hope in the moon's song? Is the world still dark?

Pilgrim: *(falters)* Well, yes, and honestly — no! The moon is bright tonight. But what of other nights? The moon is not constant like the sun. The moon comes and goes, and is brighter and darker, setting early or rising late.

Guide: The moon is like our king. The king comes and goes as he pleases. He is not tame. He is not ours to control. How we would love to stand in his light always, yet there are times he seems distant, or even hidden. But that is the way of real kings.

Pilgrim: The moon is your king?

Guide: *(gently corrects)* No, the moon is like our king. Yet nothing is like our king.

Pilgrim: And what sign can I take back to my king of this? If I cannot take the bulb with me to assure my king the world is not dying, what sign can I take that the world is not dark?

Guide: Look beneath your feet. What do you see?

Pilgrim: Nothing.

Guide: If what you see beneath your feet is nothing, then nothing is everywhere. Look again.

Pilgrim: I am standing on the earth.

Guide: What could be more solid and reassuring than the earth. The dark earth, the loam, the deep earth, where roots take hold that flowers may climb to the sun, where tall trees dig deep to drink of deeper springs?

Pilgrim: *(bends down to scoop up earth into his bag)* Then I simply have to fill my bag with the earth ...

Guide: *(interrupts)* Why? The earth is everywhere. It is here. It is past that hill. It is in your far country. It is a gift to all people everywhere from our king. You need only dig in your own country when you return. The ancient story of the earth is told and retold, and even when the moon sets and all seems dark, the earth provides cushion enough for our dreams.

Hope: *(sings)*
Dusk is erased with no hint of a morning.
Shall Hope be lost in the dark?
Not while the Moon shines to call the forlorn. Sing!
Shine in the darkness, till hark,
Day has returned, hear the lark.

Faith: *(sings)*
Faith is the hub at the heart of the flower
While in the autumn she yearns
Sweetly for spring and her nurturing shower.
Faith I am. Snow abounds. Burn.
Sunshine will always return.

Guide: Take rest yourself. Return to the castle. And later, return to me that I may answer your other concerns. For now, know that the world is not dying, the world is not truly dark. After all, even the dark is blessed and becomes a place of sleep. God is present in times of darkness. Hope is renewed again and again, by faith. After all, you don't control God.

Pilgrim: I thought you said it was your king who cannot be controlled.

Guide: Take your rest, Pilgrim. And return! In the meantime, remember these words: "For through the Spirit, by faith, we eagerly wait for the hope of righteousness" (Galatians 5:5).

Pilgrim: *(repeats)* For through the Spirit, by faith, we eagerly wait for the hope of righteousness.

Guide: For through the Spirit, by faith, we eagerly wait for the hope of righteousness.

Pilgrim: Faith and hope are tied together?

Guide: With love....

Hope: *(sings)*
Dusk is erased with no hint of a morning.
Shall Hope be lost in the dark?
Not while the Moon shines to call the forlorn. Sing!
Shine in the darkness, till hark,
Day has returned, hear the lark.

Faith: *(sings)*
Faith is the hub at the heart of the flower
While in the autumn she yearns
Sweetly for spring and her nurturing shower.
Faith I am. Snow abounds. Burn.
Sunshine will always return.

The End

Week 3
Third Week of Advent
Love: Pink Candle of the Stars

The Living Advent Wreath

(Pilgrim is standing on stage holding his empty bag. Guide enters with Love, the third candle of the living Advent wreath, who bears the mark of the Stars. Attendant, who is carrying the candlelighter to light the candles also enters. Faith and Hope enter and take their places in the living Advent wreath.)

Guide: I'm here!

Pilgrim: *(sheepishly)* I'm here, too. I guess I wanted to see you enter, to see if you would be faithful.

Guide: *(smiles)* You are not the first pilgrim who has come to our Far Country, looking for Faith and Hope, seeking reassurance. I trust your stay at the castle has been comfortable?

Pilgrim: Yes, but it has been puzzling, as well.

Guide: In what way?

Pilgrim: Everything seems orderly. Everyone seems to live under the leadership of a king. They all know their places and rejoice in their places.

Guide: And what is odd about that?

Pilgrim: Only this — that there is no king that I can see. And when I question my hosts about their king, they seem not at all alarmed about the fact that they have never seen their king, yet seem sure that he exists.

Guide: They have faith.

Pilgrim: Is faith enough?

Guide: And what did I tell you?

Pilgrim: That faith is the assurance of things hoped for, the proof of things not seen.

Guide: Exactly. And what of hope?

Pilgrim: That through the Spirit, by faith, we eagerly wait for the hope of righteousness.

Guide: Very good.

Pilgrim: If that is good enough for you, then why is it not good enough for my king and our people? My king was lying ill in his bed, certain that the world is dying, the world is dark, and the world is lost. The world is skeptical. The world is war.

Guide: And that is why you carry that bag — to bring back five things for your king to assure him he is wrong.

Pilgrim: Exactly — except that while you have demonstrated that there is hope in the bulbs hidden in the earth, and strength in the earth itself, you have given me nothing to take back as proof of the things you have taught me.

Guide: Your words will be enough, or nothing will be enough.

Pilgrim: I hope so. Yet, when I consider the depravity we witness, the cruelty of people toward each other, the dashing to dreams and the strength of evil, certainly it seems that the world is lost.

Guide: The world is not lost. People are lost.

Pilgrim: That is worse, isn't it?

Guide: The lost can be saved. You can reach them. Listen to these words of wisdom ...

Pilgrim: Will you have me look down again? Twice you have directed my attention earthward, first to the hidden bulb, which I cannot see, and then to the earth itself, which I cannot lift, nor can I take it with me. What is left earthward for me to take hope from?

Guide: No, I would direct your gaze heavenward. The sun has retreated. The moon is setting. Now look to the beacon stars and remember these words: "You will do well to be attentive to this as to a lamp shining in a dark place, until the day dawns and the morning star rises in your hearts" (2 Peter 1:19).

(Love steps forward to take the place of the third candle in the living Advent wreath as Attendant lights the first, second, and third candles in the altar's Advent wreath.)

Love: *(sings)*
Love like a star is a beacon. Believer,
Follow, tho' hounded by hates.
Love sees a pattern, and so like the weaver,
Colors bright bind us in plaits.
Patiently biding, Love waits.

Guide: The world only seems lost. There is the Sun of Faith, the Moon of Hope, and the Stars that are beacons of God's Love. The stars give guidance to the sailors at see. The stars guide those who are escaping the lash and traveling to freedom. Though the stars seem to be small, scattered lights, together they form patterns, and change the way we look at the void so that stories emerge, and with the stories, the assurance that God is unchanging, and will come again and again through the seasons of life. The stars, and this star, are a symbol of God's Love, which will not abandon the people!

Pilgrim: *(crestfallen)* Love. Is that all? What can love do, really, against the cruelty of the world?

Guide: You are confusing love with weakness. Love seems soft only to those who do not know it. But it is hard as nails — the nails that are pounded into wood. Love is bright as fire — the fire that sweeps away the brush accumulated over decades so that seeds become saplings and new trees can take root. Love is not afraid to die, but never for gain and only for others.

Pilgrim: But once again, what can I bring back? Simply the words you taught me?

Guide: You could do worse. Those words are ...

Pilgrim: *(interrupts)* You would do well to be attentive to this as to a lamp shining in a dark place, until the day dawns and the morning star rises in your hearts.

Guide: I have said that a star is a beacon. It shines brightly, faithfully over centuries. The stories that the people tell about the patterns they see in the stars are stories that do not die. Listen ...

Love: *(sings)*
Love like a star is a beacon. Believer,
Follow, tho' hounded by hates.
Love sees a pattern, and so like the weaver,
Colors bright bind us in plaits.
Patiently biding, Love waits.

Hope: *(sings)*
Dusk is erased with no hint of a morning.
Shall Hope be lost in the dark?
Not while the Moon shines to call the forlorn. Sing!
Shine in the darkness, till hark,
Day has returned, hear the lark.

Faith: *(sings)*
Faith is the hub at the heart of the flower
While in the autumn she yearns
Sweetly for spring and her nurturing shower.
Faith I am. Snow abounds. Burn.
Sunshine will always return.

Pilgrim: So you give me no star to place in my bag?

Guide: No. Like love itself, a star is too hot to contain or control. God's love burns fiercely, tearing away the illusions we share and cutting to the core of God's plan for our lives. But when you return home to your king, you will see the exact same stars in the sky. And you may point to this special star, which shines more brightly than any other — for it is a herald of something greater.

Love: *(speaks)* "But you, O Bethlehem of Ephrathah, who are one of the little clans of Judea, from you shall come forth for me one who is to rule in Israel, whose origin is from of old, from ancient days" (Micah 5:2).

Pilgrim: What does that mean?

Guide: Come once more, and you will find the answer to your king's fourth concern — for this star is a beacon that beckons to many far off, who will soon be near. And know that this star endures. Many will see it who never laid eyes on it, and will treasure its beauty although it will be hidden to their generation. But you are blessed — and know this about faith, hope, and love. They will abide, though everything else fails. And the greatest of these is ...

Pilgrim: Love, I imagine.

Guide: It is not your imagination. It is truth.

Hope: *(sings)*
Dusk is erased with no hint of a morning.
Shall Hope be lost in the dark?
Not while the Moon shines to call the forlorn. Sing!
Shine in the darkness, till hark,
Day has returned, hear the lark.

Faith: *(sings)*
Faith is the hub at the heart of the flower
While in the autumn she yearns
Sweetly for spring and her nurturing shower.
Faith I am. Snow abounds. Burn.
Sunshine will always return.

Love: *(sings)*
Love like a star is a beacon. Believer,
Follow, tho' hounded by hates.
Love sees a pattern, and so like the weaver,
Colors bright bind us in plaits.
Patiently biding, Love waits.

The End

Week 4
Fourth Week of Advent
Trust: Purple Candle of the Magi

The Living Advent Wreath

(Faith, Hope, Love, and Attendant, carrying candlelighter, enter. Trust, comprised of three people representing the magi, also enters.)

Love: *(sings)*
Love like a star is a beacon. Believer,
Follow, tho' hounded by hates.
Love sees a pattern, and so like the weaver,
Colors bright bind us in plaits.
Patiently biding, Love waits.

Hope: *(sings)*
Dusk is erased with no hint of a morning.
Shall Hope be lost in the dark?
Not while the Moon shines to call the forlorn. Sing!
Shine in the darkness, till hark,
Day has returned, hear the lark.

Faith: *(sings)*
Faith is the hub at the heart of the flower
While in the autumn she yearns
Sweetly for spring and her nurturing shower.
Faith I am. Snow abounds. Burn.
Sunshine will always return.

Trust: *(sings)*
Follow your dream in the presence of scoffers.
Choices may often seen gray.
Still we must seize what our history offers.
Star in the East lights the way.
Moon and Sun too have their say.

(Pilgrim enters with the empty bag at the same time Guide enters, but from different sides of the stage.)

Pilgrim: Faithful guide!

Guide: Pilgrim of faith!

Pilgrim: It is no longer any great task to see you and find you.

Guide: But your bag is no heavier.

Pilgrim: Still, my heart is lighter.

Guide: What will your king say? You were sent by an ailing king to bring back five things to answer his five woes — the world is ...

Pilgrim: *(interrupts)* The world is dying. The world is dark. The world is lost. The world is skeptical. The world is war. Those are the woes that trouble him. And troubled me.

Guide: No longer?

Pilgrim: What have you shown me? That the world is not dying, but resting, sleeping, waiting for a great awakening.

Guide: And not the bulbs only, waiting for the spring, but all of creation, waiting for our king to appear.

Pilgrim: You have taught me faith, though you gave me nothing for my bag.

Faith: *(sings)*
Faith is the hub at the heart of the flower
While in the autumn she yearns
Sweetly for spring and her nurturing shower.
Faith I am. Snow abounds. Burn.
Sunshine will always return.

Pilgrim: And though all seems dark, yet even at night there is the moon to cast blue shadows upon the earth itself, which is a thing of story. That gives me hope.

Hope: *(sings)*
Dusk is erased with no hint of a morning.
Shall Hope be lost in the dark?
Not while the Moon shines to call the forlorn. Sing!
Shine in the darkness, till hark,
Day has returned, hear the lark.

Guide: And though the world seems lost ...

Pilgrim: *(interrupts)* Yet there is love, more powerful than thunder and lightning, more irresistible than the movement of continents, more gentle than the fall of a snowflake, more certain than, well, even faith and hope. Like a star in the heavens, love beckons above the storms of life that rage all about us.

Love: *(sings)*
Love like a star is a beacon. Believer,
Follow, tho' hounded by hates.
Love sees a pattern, and so like the weaver,
Colors bright bind us in plaits.
Patiently biding, Love waits.

Pilgrim: So I am satisfied, even if there are no answers to a skeptical world, to a world at war. Perhaps some ills cannot be changed.

Guide: So you are content to return, even without the fulfillment of your mission?

Pilgrim: Surely faith, hope, and love are enough.

Guide: Perhaps they are. Yet, there is persistence. Even against the sneer of a skeptical world.

Pilgrim: So what sort of answers can we give to those who are not believers?

Guide: First we must not give up on such people. "God does not faint or grow weary; his understanding is unsearchable" (Isaiah 40:28). "So let us not grow weary in doing what is right, for we will reap at harvest-time, if we do not give up" (Galatians 6:9).

Pilgrim: Are these words of wisdom also from your sages?

Guide: Some people have no persistence. They will not endure in the face of what seems at first to be failure. But God is persistent, though we turn our hearts and faces from him again and again. He forgives us, seven times seventy times, and again beyond that.

Pilgrim: That is good for the creator. But who in this world shares this persistence? Who will risk all when the world scoffs?

Guide: There are those who, with only the possibility that they will see the end of God's good plan, set out in trust. Look! Here are the ones who are wise, though others consider them fools. They are the magi. They are Trust.

(Attendant lights the first, second, third, and fourth Advent candles in the Advent wreath on the altar.)

Trust: *(sings)*
Follow your dream in the presence of scoffers.
Choices may often seem gray.
Still we must seize what our history offers.
Star in the East lights the way.
Moon and Sun too have their say.

Trust: *(speaks)* We have traveled far, following the star, knowing that it leads us to the great king, the king all people seek. Our journey is nearly ended, and soon our hearts will be satisfied. But even if we are not vindicated in the eyes of others, we would still follow the star. We trust in God's goodness and glory. We trust in God's plan.

Pilgrim: *(laughs)* There is no way they will fit into my bag. The bag will remain empty. But I no longer care. I have my answer for a skeptical world. And if there is no answer to a world at war, I cannot be faulted for having traveled so far and learned so much.

Guide: Do not give up on your quest, yet! Come once more from the castle and you will learn one more thing. Bring your bag — and prepare to set out for home.

Pilgrim: Still, I doubt that you can do much about the wars and the rumors of war. They will always be among us.

Guide: What did I teach you? God does not faint or grow weary; his understanding is unsearchable (Isaiah 40:28).

Pilgrim: *(finishes)* So let us not grow weary in doing what is right, for we will reap at harvest-time, if we do not give up (Galatians 6:9).

Love: *(sings)*
Love like a star is a beacon. Believer,
Follow, tho' hounded by hates.
Love sees a pattern, and so like the weaver,
Colors bright bind us in plaits.
Patiently biding, Love waits.

Hope: *(sings)*
Dusk is erased with no hint of a morning.
Shall Hope be lost in the dark?
Not while the Moon shines to call the forlorn. Sing!
Shine in the darkness, till hark,
Day has returned, hear the lark.

Faith: *(sings)*
Faith is the hub at the heart of the flower
While in the autumn she yearns
Sweetly for spring and her nurturing shower.
Faith I am. Snow abounds. Burn.
Sunshine will always return.

Trust: *(sings)*
Follow your dream in the presence of scoffers.
Choices may often seem gray.
Still we must seize what our history offers.
Star in the East lights the way.
Moon and Sun too have their say.

The End

Week 5
Christmas Eve
The Manger: White Candle of Peace

The Living Advent Wreath

(Pilgrim and Guide enter together, followed by Faith, Hope, Love, Trust, and Attendant, who is carrying a candlelighter. Pilgrim still carries his empty bag. The curtain is closed and behind it is the manger with Mary, Joseph, and Infant.)

Pilgrim: I thank you, Guide, for all you have done for me. I came here hopeless, and now I hope to bring hope, along with faith, trust, and love to the king who sent me.

Guide: Your king had five woes — the world is dying, the world is dark, the world is lost, the world is skeptical, and the world is war.

Pilgrim: *(laughs)* And he gave me this sack to fill with five things to answer his five woes. My sack is as empty as ever, but not my heart.

Guide: What have you learned, Pilgrim, in Far Country?

Pilgrim: The world is not dying. It lives. I can see the tree has grown even as we have met! Even when it is sleeping, there is hope for the spring! As long as we have faith.

Faith: *(sings)*
Faith is the hub at the heart of the flower
While in the autumn she yearns
Sweetly for spring and her nurturing shower.
Faith I am. Snow abounds. Burn.
Sunshine will always return.

Pilgrim: The world is not dark. Even when the sun is gone, there is the light of the moon, constantly inconstant, yet bringing hope in dark places.

Hope: *(sings)*
Dusk is erased with no hint of a morning.
Shall Hope be lost in the dark?
Not while the Moon shines to call the forlorn. Sing!
Shine in the darkness, till hark,
Day has returned, hear the lark.

Pilgrim: The world is not lost. Not while there is love. Love is patient and kind. It is not jealous or boastful. It is not arrogant or rude. Certainly you were right when you said that faith, hope, and love abide, these three, and that the greatest of these is love (1 Corinthians 13:4, 13).

Love: *(sings)*
Love like a star is a beacon. Believer,
Follow, tho' hounded by hates.
Love sees a pattern, and so like the weaver,
Colors bright bind us in plaits.
Patiently biding, Love waits.

Pilgrim: Knowing the love of God helps us to trust — to follow the beacon, the star, the shining city on the hill, no matter what the skeptics might say.

Trust: *(sings)*
Follow your dream in the presence of scoffers.
Choices may often seem gray.
Still we must seize what our history offers.
Star in the East lights the way.
Moon and Sun too have their say.

Pilgrim: So, I am content now. There is no answer that can be given in the face of a world at war. The search for peace is useless.

We must make our separate peace and hope it is enough with life's dangers all around us.

Guide: Are you sure?

Pilgrim: Each time I have visited you there has been another candle to light and another song to sing. But there is no new singer here. Only Faith, Hope, Love, and Trust. I do not see Peace.

Guide: Yet, we have peace — and the promise of peace for all. That is why our wisest words remind us that, "The people who walked in darkness have seen a great light; those who lived in a land of deep darkness — on them light has shined" (Isaiah 9:2).

Pilgrim: *(looks around)* I don't see this peace.

Guide: Soon all will see it. "For all the boots of the tramping warriors and all the garments rolled in blood shall be burned as fuel for the fire. For a child has been born for us, a son given to us; authority rests upon his shoulders; and he is named Wonderful Counselor, Mighty God, Everlasting Father, Prince of Peace" (Isaiah 9:5-6). And, Pilgrim, we have this peace!

Pilgrim: *(a light is dawning)* So you are Peace?

Guide: No, I only point to it. Pilgrim, come to the manger. *(curtain opens and reveals the manger with Mary, Joseph, and Infant)* Come to the manger!

Guide: *(sings)*
What shall we say in the face of life's danger?
Come all ye faithful to me.
Though you were lost, it's not God who's the stranger.
Peace can be found with the babe in the manger.
Faith, Hope, and Love all agree.
Come to the manger and see.

Guide: Yes, yes, all is folly. We proclaim the king of peace, yet few believe in the king, and none see peace. Yet that king is surely coming. We have faith. We have hope. We share love. And we have the testimony of the wise men of the ages.

(Attendant lights all five Advent candles.)

Love, Hope, Faith, and Trust: *(sing)*
Come to the manger, ye hopeless and tired.
Shed all your cares with your greed.
Though in the wiles of worldliness mired
You may be lost — come — be freed.
God has supplied what we need.

(Each person sings a line of the song)

Love: Love like a star, is a beacon, fair stranger,
Hope: Hope will not lead you astray.
Faith: Peace can be found with the babe in the manger.
Trust: The star in the East lights the way!
All: Worship the king on this day!

Guide: "His authority shall grow continually, and there shall be endless peace for the throne of David and his kingdom. He will establish and uphold it with justice and with righteousness from this time onward and forevermore. The zeal of the Lord of hosts will do this" (Isaiah 9:7). So here is your real king, the one you must truly serve. Your worldly king is but a shadow. Here is your heart's desire. Here is your home.

Pilgrim: What difference can a baby make? And certainly I cannot take this babe back to my king!

Love, Hope, Faith, and Trust: *(sing)*
Come to the manger, ye hopeless and tired.
Shed all your cares with your greed.

Though in the wiles of worldliness mired
You may be lost — come — be freed.
God has supplied what we need.

Trust: *(sings)*
Follow your dream in the presence of scoffers.
Choices may often seem gray.
Still we must seize what our history offers.
Star in the East lights the way.
Moon and Sun too have their say.

Guide: The baby has his own path to follow. Tabernacle and temple, God is in motion. God is not still, and God is among us. There is a garden that he will weep in, a cross for him to carry, and a tomb where he will be glorified. You cannot take him with you, but you can follow him. It is not safe to do so, but it is glorious. And through him there will be peace.

"In days to come the mountain of the Lord's house shall be established as the highest of the mountains, and shall be raised up above the hills. Peoples shall stream to it,

Faith: "and many nations will come and say: 'Come, let us go up to the mountain of the Lord, to the house of the God of Jacob; that he may teach us his ways and that we may walk in his paths.' For out of Zion shall go forth instruction, and the word of the Lord from Jerusalem.

Hope: "He shall judge between many peoples, and shall arbitrate between strong nations far away; they shall beat their swords into plowshares, and their spears into pruning hooks; nation shall not lift up sword against nation, neither shall they learn war any more

Love: "but they shall all sit under their own vines and under their own fig trees, and no one shall make them afraid;

Trust: "for the mouth of the Lord of hosts has spoken" (Micah 4:1-4).

Guide: Come all ye faithful.

Guide: *(sings)*
What shall we say in the face of life's danger?
Come all ye faithful to me.
Though you were lost, it's not God who's the stranger.
Peace can be found with the babe in the manger.
Faith, Hope, and Love all agree.
Come to the manger and see.

Love: *(sings)*
Love like a star is a beacon. Believer,
Follow, tho' hounded by hates.
Love sees a pattern, and so like the weaver,
Colors bright bind us in plaits.
Patiently biding, Love waits.

Hope: *(sings)*
Dusk is erased with no hint of a morning.
Shall Hope be lost in the dark?
Not while the Moon shines to call the forlorn. Sing!
Shine in the darkness, till hark,
Day has returned, hear the lark.

Faith: *(sings)*
Faith is the hub at the heart of the flower
While in the autumn she yearns
Sweetly for spring and her nurturing shower.
Faith I am. Snow abounds. Burn.
Sunshine will always return.

Trust: *(sings)*
Follow your dream in the presence of scoffers.
Choices may often seem gray.
Still we must seize what our history offers.
Star in the East lights the way.

Moon and Sun too have their say.

Guide: Take a look in your bag, Pilgrim. If you can lift it!

Pilgrim: My bag! It is full.

(Pilgrim looks within and his bag is full. There are scrolls, a model of the Nativity, a star, a flower, and a heart.)

Guide: Do not be afraid; for see — I am bringing you good news of great joy for all the people: unto you is born this day in the city of David a Savior, who is the Messiah, the Lord. This will be a sign for you: You will find a child wrapped in bands of cloth and lying in a manger.

Pilgrim: Glory to God in the highest heaven, and on earth peace among those whom he favors! Come all ye faithful! Let us worship our king.

Guide: *(sings)*
What shall we say in the face of life's danger?
Come all ye faithful to me.
Though you were lost, it's not God who's the stranger.
Peace can be found with the babe in the manger.
Faith, Hope, and Love all agree.
Come to the manger and see.

The End

The Mouse Christmas

Note: This short play is written for a children's choir and is designed to be performed simply, with or without memorization. It is about a woman whose nativity set was ruined by a flood. All that is left is the stable and the empty manger along with some old scraps of cloth. She leaves these pieces out in sadness and walks away. The mice arrive and decide to help out by taking the parts of the characters we associate with the nativity set. Although the woman is frightened at first when she returns, she accepts the gift of the living nativity set from the mice and rewards them with a bag of seed corn.

Although some songs are indicated, the children can sing whatever songs they have already learned. Make sure that each person stands in front of a microphone and is heard clearly.

Characters

Grandmother
Outdoor Mice
Indoor Mice
Mouse King
Mouse Joseph
Mouse Cow
Mouse Pig
Mouse Angel
Mouse Shepherd
Mouse Mary
Mouse Baby

Props

Microphone
Manger
Stable
Scraps of cloth (costume parts for characters)
Bag of corn
Broom

Costumes

The children will dress as mice, probably suggested by whiskers and gray felt caps with ears. They will each don a costume piece, in turn, that transforms them into one of the characters of the nativity set.

Music

Other possible hymns not mentioned in the play that could be used are "The Virgin Mary Had A Baby Boy," "O Little Town Of Bethlehem," and "Silent Night."

(Grandmother enters with manger, stable, and scraps of cloth.)

Grandmother

Oh what a season. My basement was flooded.
My boxes were ruined when all things were mudded.
All of my boxes for Christmas were wrecked!
What will my visiting family expect?
The tree decorations, the ivy and holly,
The garlands are soggy. Things won't be too jolly.
The pieces were ruined. All I've got is the manger,
And part of the stable. Will Christmas be stranger
Because I don't have a nativity set?
Oh woe, how much sadder can all of this get?

(Grandmother exits, leaving the manger, stable, and scraps of cloth behind. Outdoor Mice and Indoor Mice enter.)

Outdoor Mice

We are the mice who live out in the barn
But come to the house for some string and some yarn
The winter is here, so we stretch and we yawn
But now we discover her set is all gone!
What on earth can we do, or else heaven can say
So Christmas can come to this woman today?

Indoor Mice
We are the mice who live left of the basement,
And freezing we huddle by bushes and casement.
Christmas means cold, but it also means Savior!
Animals celebrate by their behavior!
Let's make the manger. See what we find!
We can make costumes from scraps left behind.

(Each Mouse, in turn, takes up some scraps and dons them as a costume and recites his or her lines into the microphone.)

Mouse King
I have a present and follow the star
To seek where the hope of the world is, or are.
My grammar's uncertain, but I read the skies
And know from antiquity wherefore and whys
A king has been born, one to save the whole world!
I bring a great present that here is unfurled.

(Children sing a stanza of "We Three Kings.")

Mouse Joseph
Joseph's a carpenter. I love the wood
That gathers in shavings. It sure does taste good.
I make a nest for the mouselings to nestle,
So they can stay warm and grow up, strong to wrestle
With all that the world throws against a poor mouse.
I'll be the carpenter. I'll build the house!

Mouse Cow
Moo! I say, "Moo!" You say, "Brown cow, how now!"
We'll start conversation 'twixt me and the sow.
My straw fills the manger, and it's my dinner,
But I can share supper. I won't be much thinner.
This baby is hungry, like all of his ilk.
The least I can do is provide him some milk.

Mouse Pig
I am the pig. No offense here is taken.
But I am left out. I'm not here, ham or bacon,
When you put a manger set here on your shelf,
That's a menagerie, but not myself!
That's why I'm here. It's sort of exclusive.
Jesus saves all, he is very inclusive.

Mouse Angel
Once a cold evening love journeyed on wings.
Two thousand years and this angel still sings.
I'll share peace on earth and God's grace to all people
That seek for God's will. Let it ring from the steeple.
Gloria glory, Excelsis in Deo.
Let's look for a sandwich, I hope without mayo.

(Children sing a stanza of "It Came Upon A Midnight Clear.")

Mouse Shepherd
Maybe the folks would enjoy a fast leopard.
I am content with just being a shepherd.
I watch the sheep, and they mostly say, "Bah!"
They don't give me lip or say things like, "Yo Ma!"
When I heard the angels sing I came a running!
The sheep will take care of themselves, and no funning.
It's not very often you're there when a Savior
Is born. You don't worry about your behavior.
You run! Run as fast as your little legs can!
I may be a mouse, but for angels I ran!

(Children sing a stanza of "Angels We Have Heard On High.")

Mouse Mary
I traveled longest through wind and through snows.
I will be Mary in ribbons and bows.
God asks us all in our time, "Yes?" or "No?"
A burden to carry, a cross we might show.

It may be an honor to be the Lord's chosen
But not when you're so far from home and you're frozen.

I'll hold the baby and keep him so warm
And just like a mother protect him from harm.
From now in the present to days from of old,
So many children have suffered from cold.
Hope comes in packages small but still able.
Let's protect babies, and start in this stable.

Mouse Baby
I am the smallest, no if, but, or maybe,
And that's why I'm chosen, and I'll be the baby.
Jesus was given that long ago morn
To save us from sin, and so when he was born
The power of evil was conquered, so here
We mice have assembled and we feel no fear!

(Children sing a stanza of "What Child Is This?")

(Grandmother enters with a bag of corn. The Mice stay in place. She will take up a broom, but will stop before she strikes the mice!)

Grandmother
Eek! I see mice. Let me get out the broom
And sweep all the creatures right out of the room.
But wait — I see shepherds and angels and maybe
A king here and there, and of course here's the baby!
You've helped me to celebrate! Jesus is born!
Please take to your homes this gift of sweet corn.

All Mice
Hooray, hallelujah! We mice love your present!
This corn will make cold days seem awfully pleasant.
And we in our turn will stay out of your house
The rest of this winter. We're that kind of mouse.

Merry Christmas to all, may the Christ light shine bright,
And help everybody remember this sight.

(All sing a stanza of "Joy To The World.")

The End

The Ad Vent Wheat

Characters

Courtney
Alexis
Garrison
Bradley
Alex
Kristin
Krystal
Teacher One
Teacher Two

Props

Box labeled "Holiday Decorations"
String of Christmas lights
Nativity set
Large metal vent
Sheaves of wheat
Bag (big enough to carry the puppets)
Two hand puppets per child

(Courtney, Alexis, Garrison, Bradley, and Alex are getting ready to decorate their Sunday school classroom for Christmas. Two or three of them are dragging a big box labeled "Holiday Decorations" to the middle of the sanctuary.)

Courtney: Let's get the Sunday school classroom decorated for our teachers before they get here.

Alexis: Boy, will they be surprised!

Garrison: *(pulls out a string of lights)* Look at this! This will brighten the room.

Bradley: *(in a bossy manner)* Now you be careful. Children should never play with electricity without adults.

Garrison: Well, of course not. I will lay this aside until the teachers get here. *(holds up the nativity set)* Look here! I've got a gravity set!

Bradley: Don't be silly. That's not a gravity set. That's a nativity set!

Garrison: Then how come when I drop it *(drops it)* it falls? I think it's a gravity set.

Alex: What's a gravity set for?

Courtney: It's for the Baby Jesus! We put in the manger, see? And the Baby Jesus!

Alexis: And Mary and Joseph!

Bradley: And sheep and cows!

Garrison: And the angel and the star!

Bradley: This is how we tell the Christmas story!

Courtney: And don't forget the wise guys!

Bradley: You mean the wise men!

Courtney: No, I mean the wise guys — Kristin and Krystal. They're not here yet. Where are they?

(Kristin and Krystal enter dragging a large metal vent along with some sheaves of wheat.)

Kristin: Here we are!

Krystal: We're coming! Help us with this stuff.

(The other children help Kristin and Krystal bring the stuff they are dragging over to the middle of the sanctuary. They lay it down in front and all pause to catch their breath.)

Garrison: What is this for?

Krystal: This is the Ad Vent!

Kristin: And this is the Ad Vent Wheat!

Courtney: What?

Krystal: The grown-ups are talking all about Ad Vent. They say it is the time to get ready for Christmas.

Kristin: Advertisements are the way we tell people about things. And we call them "Ads" for short.

Krystal: And we're going to show our Ads through this Vent. That's why they call it Ad — Vent!

Kristin: And you're supposed to have an Ad Vent Wheat.

Alexis: Why?

Kristin: *(shrugs shoulders)* Maybe so the Baby Jesus has some bread to eat.

Garrison: I love fresh bread!

Alex: Let's try out the Ad Vent with our pudding song. Pudding is like bread!

All: *(sing into the Ad Vent)*
We wish you a Merry Christmas.
We wish you a Merry Christmas.
We wish you a Merry Christmas,
And a Happy New Year.

We all want some figgy pudding.
We all want some figgy pudding.
We all want some figgy pudding,
So bring it right here.

We won't go until we get some.
We won't go until we get some.
We won't go until we get some,
And a cup of good cheer.

We wish you a Merry Christmas.
We wish you a Merry Christmas.
We wish you a Merry Christmas,
And a Happy New Year.

Garrison: This Ad Vent works pretty good. What other Ads do we want to get out this Christmas?

Courtney: Well, Christmas is about the Baby Jesus. We need to remind the grown-ups of that.

Bradley: Yeah. All they do is shop and cook, and sometimes they get very grumpy. And Christmas is not about the Baby Grumpy.

Alexis: Yeah, Grumpy was a dwarf, not a baby.

Krystal: I'll bet he was a baby dwarf once upon a time.

Alexis: So what song can we sing about the Baby Jesus?

Garrison: You know, when a baby is born, they always weigh them. Let's sing the song about how much Jesus weighs.

Kristin: What song is that?

Garrison: "A Weigh In The Manger." They weighed the Baby Jesus and put him in the manger. Only they don't tell us how much he weighed.

All: *(sing)*
Away in the manger, no crib for a bed,
The little Lord Jesus laid down his sweet head.
The stars in the sky looked down where he lay,
The little Lord Jesus asleep on the hay.

The cattle are lowing, the baby awakes,
But Little Lord Jesus no crying he makes.
I love thee, Lord Jesus! Look down from the sky,
And stay by my side until morning is nigh.

Be near me, Lord Jesus, I ask thee to stay
Close by me forever, and love me, I pray.
Bless all the dear children in thy tender care,
And fit us for heaven to live with thee there.

Courtney: This advertising thing isn't so bad. The grown-ups are going to love this.

Kristin: Now, one thing an Ad has to do is make sure everyone knows the whole story. So we need to sing a song that tells the whole story.

Courtney: That's easy. Let's do "The Virgin Mary Had A Baby Boy!" It tells us about the baby and the angel and the wise guys.

Bradley: Wise men!

Courtney: Wise guys. Did you take a look at the gravity set? *(holds up a wise man)* These guys are dressed pretty funny.

All: *(sing)*
Silent night, holy night, all is calm, all is bright
round yon virgin mother and child. Holy infant, so tender and mild,
sleep in heavenly peace, sleep in heavenly peace.

Silent night, holy night, shepherds quake at the sight;
glories stream from heaven afar, heavenly hosts sing alleluia!
Christ the Savior is born, Christ the Savior is born.

Silent night, holy night, Son of God, love's pure light;
radiant beams from thy holy face with the dawn of redeeming grace,
Jesus, Lord at thy birth, Jesus, Lord, at thy birth.

Silent night, holy night, wondrous star, lend thy light;
with the angels let us sing, Alleluia to our King;
Christ the Savior is born, Christ the Savior is born!

(Teachers enter during the last song. They clap when the song is over. Teacher Two carries a bag filled with the puppets.)

Teacher One: Very good! I'm impressed.

Teacher Two: And the decorations are so nice. But what is this big metal shaft? And why do you have this wheat here?

Alexis: This is the Ad Vent!

Kristin: We want to tell the whole world about Jesus, so we're telling our Ads through this Vent.

Krystal: And this is our Ad Vent Wheat! We want to share God's bread with the Baby Jesus and all the people who are hungry.

Teacher One: Children, I'm not sure if you quite understand about Advent and the Advent Wreath.

Teacher Two: Now wait a minute. Aren't we supposed to tell people about Jesus? And aren't we supposed to share the Bread of Life with everyone?

Teacher One: You're right. They may be onto something, don't you think? Children, did you know that Bethlehem is where Jesus was born, and the word "Bethlehem" means "house of bread"?

Courtney: Maybe it means "house of big metal vent," also.

Teacher Two: Maybe. Well, if you want to tell people about Jesus, what should we say?

Alexis: We should say, "Be happy!"

Bradley: Joy to everyone!

Garrison: And we should bring all our friends to Baby Jesus, too.

Teacher One: Well, guess what? I brought some friends with me. *(takes the puppets out of the bag and hands them out, giving each child one for each hand)* Now we can all sing together.

(Everyone puts on their hand puppets.)

Teacher Two: Let's get everyone here in the church to sing with us, as well! Won't you?

Cast Members and Congregation: *(sing)*
Joy to the world, the Lord is come,
Let earth receive her king.
Let every heart prepare him room.

And heaven and nature sing.
And heaven and nature sing.
And heaven and heaven and nature sing.

Joy to the earth, the Savior reigns!
Let all their songs employ.
While fields and floods,
Rocks, hills, and plains
Repeat the sounding joy
Repeat the sounding joy
Repeat, repeat the sounding joy.

No more let sings and sorrows grow,
Nor thorns infest the ground.
He comes to make his blessings flow
Far as the curse is found.
Far as the curse is found,
Far as, far as the curse is found.

He rules the world with truth and grace,
And makes the nations prove
The glories of his righteousness
And wonders of his love.
And wonders of his love
And wonders, and wonders of his love.

The End

www.ingramcontent.com/pod-product-compliance
Lightning Source LLC
LaVergne TN
LVHW010543100826
845148LV00013B/2581

* 9 7 8 0 7 8 8 0 2 4 8 5 6 *